Two Green Parrots

Also by Anne M Carson

Writing on the Wall, Mark Time Books, 2017
Removing the Kimono, Hybrid Publishers, Melbourne, 2013
The Sounds of Colour: The stories of mothers of and workers with children on the Autism Spectrum (editor), Kew Neighbourhood Learning Centre 2013,
Kaleidoscope, Autism through the Eyes of Mothers (editor), In Spectrum, Melbourne, 2012
Espresso Chapbook (editor), Kew Neighbourhood Learning Centre, 2012
Choices From the Heart: A Collection of Stories (editor), Kew Neighbourhood Learning Centre, 2012

Anne M Carson

Two Green Parrots

To dearest Julian and Alison: partner and friend,

incomparable companions –

Taureans both, who keep me anchored.

Two Green Parrots
ISBN 978 1 76041 715 4
Copyright © text Anne M. Carson 2019
Cover image © Brenda Gael Smith: *Flying Colours: King Parrot*,
2013 (textile painting) – http://brendagaelsmith.com/

First published 2019 by
GINNINDERRA PRESS
PO Box 3461 Port Adelaide 5015 Australia
www.ginninderrapress.com.au

Contents

Prologue	7
On being taken there	9
I	11
Yula: The return	13
Two green parrots	14
Black Kites	15
Wattle Birds, Kew	17
Swiftlet Hotel	18
Cockatoo: a cautionary	20
In circlets of dusky light	22
Heaven's embroidered cloths	23
Golden every wych way	24
Golden ash art	25
Gone, the mother-tree	26
Going to the holy trees	28
Aboreal sorority	29
Old friends, three elementals	31
Vintage song	32
Harvesting sweet pea seeds	34
Cloud combing	35
Morning glory cloud	36
Matti ka attar	38
Before day's push and grab	39
The marmalade fox	40
II	41
Axiology	43
The river beneath, remembered	44
:meditations on melancholy	45
Pocket and Seed	46

Exuviate 2: Where Have All the Children Gone?	47
The empty chairs	48
Bodies remembering war	50
Poem without Huckleberry in it	51
Traveller's fantasy in Washington DC	52
john and yoko meet for the first time	53
The artist removes the *kopi* of mourning	54
Mother-stone is womb	56
After Listening to a Ceremony of Carols	58
Heaven backwards	59
At my father's funeral	60
L'informateur	61
From the temple's mouth	62
This amplitude	64
An assay on intimacy	65
The hug	66
Bach and the essence of things	67
Playing the Soft-loud	69
The filament of the body	72
Riding back in the dusk	73
The ghost of an argument	74
Calling the world into being	75
Embarking together	77

Epilogue   79
     (   )   81

Notes   82

Acknowledgements   83

Prologue

On being taken there

Anything can take you there –
today it is the clip-clop percussion

of horse's hooves as they strike
bitumen. The sounds ring out

resplendent, a melody the horse
makes from the marriage between

pastern, canon bones
and ground. Not just the resonant

clang of metal striking metal
but all the grace of gallop

and canter is there embryonic
in the sound and its tattooed rhythm.

The symphony which plays
when horse gathers musculature

and will to thunder across pasture,
to flash equine into the world.

I

Yula: The return

Shearwaters (mutton birds), Phillip Island, Victoria

A single dim shape shoots out of the dusk behind us
carrying deeper darkness on its wings and the imprint

of stars, snow, the never-ending night flight. More birds
follow – leaves blown by a gale. They slip over the lip

of the land, down the cliff-face like children down
a slide. The flock wheels over the water; patches of ink

in the sky clotting and dissolving like liquid stirred
into watercolour. Intricate Rorschach patterns emerge

and retreat – the curve of a blade, a bill. Uncanny
quiet descends, closes us into a cone of silence

with them. There are so many birds their wingbeats
are palpable in the dark – a cauldron of movement

above the bay. And the young, tucked into underground
bunkers, defenceless against encroaching

night. Thousands of solitary chicks alone, waiting,
hungry mouths open – calling, calling, calling.

Two green parrots

Two green parrots wing across a granite sky.
Grief and hope together again, as close
as fingers on a hand, feathers on a wing.

They don't fly straight, as arrows do
into a standing target, they are not ammunition
fired out of the sky's maw. They dip and rise,

weaving muscle and delight into strands
of effortless grace, calling as they go.
What do humans know of the calls of birds?

But it sounds like liquid pleasure, it sounds
like they laugh and make merry against
the backdrop of the approaching storm.

Black Kites

Milvus migrans, Broome

Airborne black kites poise
    on thermals
    strung out in a momentary line
    across the bluff

They work to keep balance
    bob like corks on a net
    mirroring the row of surfers out at the break
    waiting for the tide to turn

Two veer from the flock
    fly adjacent spirals
    One rising looks like it causes the other to fall
    a kind of aerial hydraulics

Seamless circles interlock into figure eights
    Perfect lazy synchrony
    but for one mismatched moment
    a mere wingtip lift corrects
    Mastery restored
    the bird rises on a spire of light

Fluent in the syntax of flight
    the articulation of bone-knit with sinew
    they know how velocity is wrought
    from feather flex and tilt

The grace of the bird is legion
        a never-grown-old liturgy
        tracing tawny sky-mandalas
        gliding on invisible currents
        resting on pillars of air

Another melds to the element
        becomes one with breath-gust
        emptying as it falls into grace
        a tossed tatter of cloth
        taken by gravity

An outrider dives into infinity
        pivots at the last moment
        drops like a harrier jet, to claw bread
        from a child's astonished hands

In the space where human meets wild
        the birds strip repose from the day
        The tails of these birds fork
        waiting for death, feeding on life

Wattle Birds, Kew

Anthochaera carunculata

Wattle birds wake up raucous.
>They don't murmur their way into day
>or carol the growing light.
>They ram their voices into the first chink
>that opens between dark and dawn, staking claims.
>Voice as lever, they wrench morning open for themselves.

Outside my bedroom a family group seizes control
>from the coo coo of doves,
>the silver whisper of birch leaves.
>Skylarking, they chase pals
>from branch to branch, band together
>to screech noisy miners from their patch.

Oblivious of niceties, they shake their wattles
>like fists at morning light, at other birds.
>They rattle their voice box, till stone-filled warnings
>clatter from their throats. Three times the birds knock
>guttural gavels against silence. Toc-toc-toc rings out,
>piercing peace's membrane,
>hacking glottal pronouncements up like phlegm
>spat into night-cleansed day.

Their dawn jargon is an abrasive loop of verbal assault,
>muscling into morning, not with force or weapons
>but with sounds strafed from gunmetal throats;
>vocal shrapnel lobbed into day.
>6 a.m.: already ugliness.

Swiftlet Hotel

Malaysia

To cook *yan wa*, soak then steam eight nests for three – four hours, remove foreign matter, add clarified chicken stock.

Dark sky-smudges announce the flock,
hundreds wheeling, feeding on the
wing. They enter as a flurry of black

darts shot from a blowgun, quicker than
the eye grasps. Tiny tapered wings –
each wingbeat displaces multiple small

scoopfuls of air. Purpose built, multistorey
concrete shells mimic caves –
a matrix of wooden beams, carefully

placed nooks for nesting. Piped birdsong,
ventilation – cacophonous. Swiftlets make
very bad neighbours. They throw clicks

out like white canes; judging distance,
contour, navigating in split-second aerial
gymnastics. Clinging to the wall with his

toes, beak as bobbin, the male weaves
strands of saliva into delicate semi-transparent
bone-china cups. His nest has no leaves,

feathers, straw or twigs, almost entirely
woven of solidified spit. Two even three
nests are harvested each season – his hotel

tariff – but the birds come again and again,
entering and leaving as they please, populations
explode. The best hotels are never empty.

Cockatoo: a cautionary

Driving the trance-inducing, serpentine road, each
curve known to the body rhythmically, kinesthetically.
Morning at-oneness explodes with a commotion

of cockatoos. A whole flock flung across the road,
the verge; lifting, flapping, flustered like scatters of
ripped cloth roused by a gale. Braking, I obey them

as if traffic cops divert cars round an accident. Closer;
screech lifts to crescendo and the flock lifts clear.
A flurry of wings – whiteness fletched with sulphur

yellow. In overhanging gums, they warn with rapier
rasps deep in their throats, menacing, wild music.
One scrap of bird is left behind, nothing obviously

wrong, no blood or gore. I approach on foot, on guard,
scores of eyes eagling my every. I talk, hope my tone
conveys lack of threat, desire to help. I weigh the

unknown imponderables against the mercy of the day,
retrieve a blanket from the boot. Feeling foolish I give
the watching birds the courtesy of an explanation,

needing to account to them. The bird doesn't flinch
when I lift it into the car, squeeze with it behind the
steering wheel, not even when I lower it onto my

cautious lap. I imagine us into a pocket of camaraderie,
fantasise I have crossed the wild animal divide with
only earnest goodwill. I carry the bird through the

vet's door, am ushered straight to surgery. Before I can
remove confining hands it wakes suddenly from stupor,
grabs the closest threat with black metal beak, strong

as pliers. I try to remove my bloody finger, ripping the
membrane of cosy understanding I thought we shared.
The vet shames me into painful silence. I leave shaking –

my wrongness graphic in images of frenzied feathers,
scythe-like, fear-fuelled slashes in the confinement
of the car…the risk I have taken. On the way home

I stop where birds remain on vigil, white flags the trees
proffer. They have unwillingly surrendered a flock member.
The bird will stay away overnight I tell them, be helped,

I hope. All I hear is their warning rasp – scratching away
at what's left coherent in my day. The vet rings in the
morning to say the bird has died overnight, in a cage

under black cloth, alone. *They rarely recover*, she says,
softening since the bird no longer suffers. *It's the shock
which gets them.* I'll never know if it was the accident

or being confined. I take my well-meaning ignorance
to where it all started, under the gums, branches empty
of knowledge. They bow towards the earth, denuded

now of birds. I send the sombre colours of my apology
out to the absent flock with their missing member,
to the wide open sky, to the empty, listening trees.

In circlets of dusky light

Cape lilac: *Melia azedarach*

The Cape lilacs have come into bloom, exhaling their
scent into the night air. They breathe for us; take in poison,
give back perfume, spicing suburbia with the fragrance
of Persia though we're half a world away.

You're still here, though we feared you wouldn't last
past the time when berries were bare on the branch;
polished hard like wooden beads, secular rosaries for
a modern world. That was the stark part of the cycle
when there was only acquiescence.

A time not without beauty; the tree's winter silhouette
cut a fine figure against dusk in a Maxfield Parrish way –
turned statuesque by lighting. Members of the mahogany
family – fine-grained, durable beauty.

Under the shadow of uncertainty you cleave to courage,
confidence you are loved, faith you will be looked after
to the end. You have acquired the equanimity that trees
have, grace under pressure as branches bend without
breaking when wind is heavy.

Cape lilacs burst first into bud, then leaf. Now they're
in the flush of a full complement – leaves, blossom-clusters
of pale purple stars, some renegades still clutching
their china-berries. The flowers halo the trees in circlets
of dusky lilac light – ordinary, everyday immanence made
tangible. And you still with us.

Heaven's embroidered cloths

Jacaranda mimosifolia – after Yeats

The jacaranda is an openwork botanical
stitched onto the world's parachute ceiling.

Raised scallops and picots are three-dimensional
ornaments – heavily patterned

threadwork weighing down the fabric of the sky.
Today it's a shot silk of greys and mother-of-pearl,

embroidered with unpindownable jacaranda
blue. Gorgeous purple-blue, agapanthus-toned.

Cut a panel from the sky to sew a ruff onto
your doublet, another to trim the cuffs

of your smock. Feel the reassuring weight
of quality handwork fall around your wrists,

rest confidingly against your throat, your chest,
feel the swing of the hem. Flower-lace with

enough substance to pull heaven earthwards,
permitting exquisite tastes of paradise.

Golden every wych way

Golden wych elm: *Ulmus glabra Lutescens*

Each leaf is a lens filtering light into the tree's
ample aura; taffeta greens shot through with

clean citrus tones. Foliage that steps the sun
down into wattage soft and soothing enough

to do you good. Just to look is botanical
baptism. Behind the new leaves are older,

darker leaves; deep bottle-green which cup
new growth the way a florist cuffs flowers

in a posy – darker outlines lending depth,
definition, three dimensionality. A comely

arrangement by someone who knows her
aesthetics – symmetry, balance, how to use

shadow so the feature stands out. The light
and the dark of leaves is a philosophy the tree

imparts; the new coming into being, the old
falling away, no longer in the limelight.

Golden ash art

The tree is restoration green,
canopy like a giant café

umbrella – plenty of reach
and give under its branches,

the gift of a generous shade.
I never look up into the crown

always down to the ground
to the tree's multiple signatures

scrawled in the once-wet
concrete below. Two panels

of cement decorated with
a scatter of delicately stencilled

leaves, a filigree of stems
and stalks, even the dendritic

trail of veins. William Morris
wallpaper or a Japanese screen,

laid underfoot for pedestrians'
pleasure. The turning

of a functional footpath –
aesthetic – thanks to the tree's

innate artistry and a conversation
it had with the breeze.

Gone, the mother-tree

Golden ash: *Fraxinus excelsior 'Aurea'*

Under the arms of the silver birch I find another diminutive
forest of golden ash seedlings, a spreading bonsai understorey,
taken root. I pull them out, one after the other,

feeling the stem's wiry strength, the moment of grip before
release, how life hangs on. They colonise all corners of the
garden, any foothold offering purchase. Every few weeks

more miniature plantations, another crop hidden under
seaside daisies, by the acanthus clump. Only since the
mother-tree came down, not before. How do they know?

It was not the tree's fault that the neighbour's storm water
masqueraded as underground watercourse, pulling roots
irresistibly. Fault or not, the tree was felled. Not how they

used to bring trees down – battle with worthy adversary,
necessity of brute strength then the dreadful glory of an
almighty crash, sound ringing out through the forest –

sound commensurate with act. This is piecemeal
dismemberment with no honour in it. I can hardly watch.
The night before the loppers arrive I go out for farewell,

for warning, as if the tree could suck its life force back into
the earth somehow, protect itself from the chainsaw's teeth.
I put palms to bark, rest my forehead against strength.

Acquiescence to the inevitable. I grieve for the grandeur
of the tree, gift of cool summer canopy, arabesque of arms
in winter, palette of coloured leaves painted on autumn sky.

The offspring are charged with the challenge of life. Months
pass; still they slip periscopes through soil, reaching for life
and when I'm not looking, they unfurl another green banner.

Going to the holy trees

Based on a series of photographs, *Night Watch*, by Elif Sezen

Vibrant ultraviolet blue shapes printed onto
silk, fine enough to see the delicate pink scrawl
of capillaries, veins. Hung on the slender, pale

trunks of gum trees. Images of organs – brain,
stomach with its spiral of intestines, heart, the
familiar peanut curve of kidney. Attached to

the trees the way they hang wafer-thin tin *Milagros*
in Mexico. The likeness of limb, organ, heart
stamped on metal, dangling from statues and

icons of saints. Churches glint with their coded
metal messages, their multiple heartfelt SOSs.
People's pleas made manifest, made beautiful.

You go to trees like this, as if they were holy,
as if they were saints capable of bestowing
blessings. You tell us that the organs vibrate

with the memory of pain. You invite the universal
perfection of nature to touch and to heal. How
exposed the organs look without the body's skin

garment to protect them. The vulnerable foetal-
curled kidney attached cicada-like, the way
young cling to a mother's back. You have put

them within a eucalyptus aura, under the aegis
of green, left them to the ministration of sun and
moon, the intercession of the doctoring wind.

Old friends, three elementals

Lake Takepo, McKenzie Basin, South Island, New Zealand

The wind picks up, playing the pines by the lake-shore – delicate
fingers across filaments. Today they sing a plaintive song, Aeolian
lament to the body of water they have lived by for so long. It's not

always like that – when the sun shines and turns the lake translucent,
sometimes the wind whips up wavelets – then the trees are loud
with vigour and exclamation. They are old friends, three elementals –

though the wind is a gypsy-spirit and the water an alchemist.
They are familiars, familiar with each other's moods, each other's
histories; ease of connection emerging from long-standing proximity,

the repetitiveness of daily life. Sometimes the lake dredges up the past;
plunging, writhing, frozen heart. It gets fractious, tosses in its bed,
then settles again into the habit of placidity, the pleasure of flow.

It retains the glorious turquoise depths of its glacial past, losing only
solidity in exchange for freedom of expression. Always an equilibrium
between the three, moving out of, then back into balance again.

Arboreal sorority

Crepe myrtles: *Lagerstroemia*
Cape chestnuts: *Calodendrum capense*

The party girls have tarted themselves up
for a night out again – nail polish & lippy

to match, party frocks from their colour
coordinated closets in shades of pink

and puce, flaunting their flounces and
finery. Taut tan limbs under their skirts

are bared to the season. Exuberant to
have an occasion to swan about. They

know how good they look against an
azure sky, pose there to be admired,

showing their outfit to advantage.
Good-time girls, pleasing only themselves.

*

The chestnuts are more pretty than party.
Frills and ruffles add a soft feminine touch.

Today they've donned pink ribbons and
braid inked with magenta dots, tying their

petals into bows. They don't need a reason
but they do have summer to celebrate.

Summer with blue skies and other
perfections. They like to display themselves,

court compliments, but theirs is a refined
gaiety – decorous, restrained.

Vintage song

St Andrews, Victoria

Grapes move inexorably towards ripeness. Inside the berry,
behind its fleshy walls – the mechanics of veraison. Acid

levels fall, sugars rise, the flesh dehydrates, phenols and
tannins grow fat with flavour. Little factory, humming

with alchemy, broadcasting musky perfume into the autumn
air, wave after waft of sweet enticement. The aromas

are streamers the fruit unfurls, festooning the vineyard
with the intoxicating odours of harvest. Once grapes

were blessed before vintage, a priest in regalia sprinkled
holy water over the vines. Vestiges remain of the blessèd

grape; mythic presence, thrum of spirit. Festivities
celebrate the crop – laden tables adorned with grape-leaf

foliage, glasses boasting previous vintages, friends proposing
toasts. Happiness to have the harvest home. Before the feast –

the delicate balance of sugar levels and picking-friendly
weather. Humans are on hand with measuring devices

and daily readings; instruments and science pick the exact
moment. Birds discern the perfect timing for their forays with

only aroma to guide them – fine natural viticulturists regardless
of weather. Flocks fly in early with special picking teams,

preferring their grapes on the tart side of sweet. Scores of silver
eyes find tears in the nets, waiting in orderly aerial queues like

planes in airport landing patterns, cooperative and collision-free
without traffic control. Bird after patient bird flies through

holes smaller than a child's fist, keeping entries separate from
exits. Vociferous local gang gangs troupe in for the day, return

home to roost each night. Pied currawongs become familiars
in dailiness, arriving en masse to take up temporary residence.

They dress in formal robes, decorate dusty paths with
brilliant blood-red splats studded with ruby gems; startling

splotches of colour which brighten the dull dun and tan bush.
They announce the season, the readiness of the crop. A single

bird initiates the call, anticipates antiphonal response. It rings
out onomatopoeic; *currrawong, currawong, currawong.*

Volleys of sound echo the valley; dawn greetings warbled
into pristine cold mornings, chansons chanted into crisp

skinned days, solos sung into the descending chill of dusk:
beautiful, haunting. Each phrase tapers to eerie vibrato,

finishes with rising intonation. In secular times, the birds
offer the vineyard the simple grace of choral benediction.

Harvesting sweet pea seeds

after reading May Swenson

stiff crumpled clothes the plant has
lived in   ready to discard   ready

to turn to dust   all the green gone
the growing done   pods brittle in

the hand   bony vein and spine
ridges   tendrils once muscular

spiral in on themselves   dried to
desiccation   arabesques of arrested

movement   sharp bursts of sound
cut through the garden silence

surprisingly loud   inside the papery
pods   delicate with hairs   seeds

rat-a-tat   a sound not green
but bone   bleached and blonded

past colour   miniature gunshots
voicing death   they rattle in their

pod   shake in their shell   embryos
tap-tap-tapping against the walls

the new within the old   the living
within the dead   the call for release

Cloud combing

Near Marropna Caves, Tasmania

It's been a hard night.
Morning finds the sky

in disarray, massed with
cloud-knots and snarls.

Once-fine strands of
stratus are now matted,

messy. The wind gets to
work with its wide-toothed

comb, working the snags
free, patient, persistent.

By mid-afternoon gentle
order is restored. Wispy

tendrils fan out from
the crown, long kinked

tresses cascade, catching
last glints of sun.

Morning glory cloud

Roll-cloud, Bateman's Bay, NSW

The front comes in from the west
dimming light like cloth thrown
over the lamp   dousing us
in early dark   Thunder blasts off
the cliff walls announcing
a massive white cloud   twenty
kilometres long   one hundred
and fifty metres high unrolling
over the bay   Like ancients
we don't know what it means
only that it vibrates with portent
The cloud-body quickens over
the tops of the spotted gums
spins a slow cylinder   furling
out over the water   Wisps
of vapour feather from it   burn
cold like dry ice   Its reach
stretches credulity   from beyond
the South Head of Malua Bay
over Tollgate Islands all the way
to Batehaven   A rolling roiling
cloud-mass smoothed into
softly rounded peaks   Billions
of whizzing moisture particles
cohere into a single discrete
cloud-shape   edges picked
out cleanly by remnant sunlight

The tube turns on its axis
towards us   as stately
as the slow revolve of a huge
creature held aloft in a wet cradle
It moves away from us still
revolving in balletic grace
its long arm sweeps an arabesque
across the bay into the straits
Its tail disappears into the gunmetal
grey mouth of storm clouds
Behind a nimbus of light flares
an augury we still don't know
how to interpret

Matti ka attar

Earth perfume

Longed for prelude to end-of-drought drenching –
the unforgettable smell of rain on the air. Dusty, fresh,

full of hope-fat ozone. Relief-bringer, happiness-giver.
An oily attar trapped in soil and stone, freed by moisture

in humidity before a downpour. As if the rock itself
weeps, cries in desperate relief. Aerosols carry the aromatics.

Thirsty cattle lift their heavy heads, stir from torpor to smell
promise on the scent-laden air. The celebratory fizz of release,

odour-rich particles carried on the wings of the four winds.
Blessed by the gods – *Petrichor* – essence of earth.

Before day's push and grab

Before day's push and grab
before other sounds compromise

the perfect quiet, the bird

throws its voice into the void
Its turn for morning soliloquy.

The marmalade fox

The fur on the marmalade fox is as bright as the jam
sent back to Paris from the orange groves of Marrakesh.
The globes of thousands of Moroccan suns squeezed into
jars. All that compressed bitterness and sweetness
casbahs the colour. Hold a jar up to the light, see the
amber translucence.

                So much life still in him, dead and
maggoty by the side of the road. Wind riffles his fur, sun
combs his marmalade coat. A fox stands on the verge
waiting for a gap in traffic. The marmalade fox is a thought
fox.

II

Axiology

If I was ceramic I'd be *kintsukuroi*,
pottery which has been knocked,
dropped, broken into shards then
mended with gold or silver lacquer,
a delicate meander of liquid gold
flowing into the breach. *Kintsukuroi* –
the word a whole world, evoking
the kind of place where mending
is valued more than the break,
where old is treasured more than
new, where putting things back
together is an art form, things more
beautiful for having been broken.

The river beneath, remembered

Hawkesbury River, NSW, Australia

When we begin our crossing, the river is a black impenetrable box
oars ratchet across. The water with its denizens, the shape-changing

night; closed to me. Heat stings my shoulders, evening lowers its hood,
and sunlight gashes the horizon – a wound leaking. The adults gush

and grin in newfound bonhomie, friends formed in the proximity
of seat-sharing, the socialism of touch; helping hand to elbow.

Huddled within the safety of a scowl, a pimply disguise, I practise
sullen, buy myself a private corner in which to be alone with my secret

life. Between blanketing sky and riverbed, evening seeps in, like the tide
returning. Imagination claims its realm; monarch. An underground river

flows beneath the adult world, out of sight, never conceived by them.
The boat carries us across the deep, home to prodigal creatures: bivalves

opening and closing doors of welcome and repulse, crustaceans, sleek
silver-backed fish, and squid like diaphanous ball gowns, floating billowy

and elegant, in slow processional along mythic waterways. Fish bones
and debris nestle in darkness on the muddy floor, weightless, stirred to slow,

ghostly dance. The river exhales fishy, briny breath; replete. Becoming
luminous in memory, that louvred night; oblongs of pale reflected light.

:meditations on melancholy

You said melancholy, I said Chopin;
a poultice you could put on pain.

Dark notes held by beauty in a soft hand.
Not cry-your-eyes out, slumped in blurs

of despond. But clear-eyed chords;
elegiac philosophy carried on rivers

of soul. Comfort for the bloody business
of loss, the carnage of having what is

as close to you as your own limb lopped.
The nocturnes lasso darkness with light;

ever-widening stories to which
your tale belongs. The simple peace

when pain is consented to.
Silos of silence to sink into.

Pocket and Seed

i.m. Lindsay D'arth, 21.9.55–29.9.81

He'd given up smoking, said the desire
for nicotine had seeped from his body
of its own accord. But he sucked
smoke from the exhaust pipe like his
lungs craved it, his life depended on it.
I heard it from his father, voice hoarse
with devastation like ground harrowed
by the plough.

                It wasn't until that very
moment that I found a small hard seed
inside me too, tucked in an inside pocket,
kept even from myself. I didn't know I
had it in me, pocket or seed. The pact I
made that day – the only thing I had big
enough to make a difference. His death
meant I could never take my own.

Exuviate 2: Where Have All the Children Gone?

Installation by Jin Nu at White Rabbit Gallery, Sydney, January 2012

Exuviate: to shed

One small garment for each two million, five hundred thousand killed. Twenty semi-transparent, starched silk dresses no bigger than a two-year-old. Frilled, yoked, pinafored, puff-sleeved. Suspended from the ceiling by invisible thread; gossamer sparkles when light picks out gold in the weave. The dresses puff out, twirl gentle pirouettes when the spirit-girls come to play – pale wraiths, willowy limbs, the suggestion of laughter. At the whim of the wind, once at the whim of the state. The dress is a skin shed after the body has gone. It remembers body's shape just as womb remembers, heart remembers.

The empty chairs

An installation by Peter Majendie, 2013, Christchurch, New Zealand

What you notice first is the absence of bustle – no briefcase-wielding,
backpack-wearing throng, no bicycles or buses
moving with purpose and resolve about a busy CBD.

A whole city, without mercy, to its knees.

Instead, awed, eerie silence in front of ruin, rubble.
Two years on and you still see tears and embraces, floral
tributes, even a mad prophet gesticulating outside the cathedral.

He thinks it's biblical and he's right but only in magnitude.
Space looms where you know it has no right to, loud with
buildings which once were. A deconstructed city, learning

how to hold itself, how to put itself together again, from scratch.

Scaffolding, hoarding, propped up facades, fences around
red zones, witches' hats confining long streams of traffic
to rumination pace. An occasional solitary building still stands.

Mountains of debris, mountains of empty space.

Absence reverberates at every site.

Artists' efforts everywhere in evidence, their quirk
and talent, lateral ways of seeing, adding value to communal
enterprise. Mending what is rent, tending what is frayed.

Floral, graphic, multimedia installations, designers reimagining
the city, making it possible for people again. Pop-ups
and start-ups; strange new growth the city has never seen before.

The eternal marrying of creation and destruction.

On a patch of reclaimed land, behind the Cardboard Cathedral,
a backdrop of cloth words woven into the wire. Sombre coloured
neckties spell out F-A-I-T-H, a stretch even to conceive of it.

Scarves in vibrant colours declare L-O-V-E and H-O-P-E,
garlanded with fabric flowers. Make-shift art, ready to spring
into spaces desperate for it. The task of artists – to keep

their eyes open, no matter what.

On a patch of grass nearby, one hundred and eighty-five
empty chairs, one for each person who perished. Baby capsule,
child's school chair, wheelchair, straight-backed wooden

kitchen seats, large wing-backed cane chair – stark, poster-paint
white, ordinary and eccentric side by side.
Like the one at home they won't come back to.

Each chair gaping a yawning hole of loss

like the lap of the beloved, forever empty.

Row on row – a witness of chairs open to the elements –
an ordered array, corralling what can't ever be ordered
or arrayed. But remembered, honoured.

Bodies remembering war

After *Afghanistan*, an exhibition by Ben Quilty, war artist, 2011

he paints the soldiers naked   they fling flail flop
across his canvas   bodies imprinted with the death
of dying comrades   he brings vulnerability out

from where it is hidden under uniform   they are still
but their remembering bodies are full of motion
evidence of bullet-rip   mortar-blast   convulsion

of organ   bone-shatter   bodies gashed open
thick with the hideous innards of the war machine
the dangling guts of human despair spilled onto canvas

the anguish of war in colours of blood and bruise
carcasses in the butcher's shop hung on the hook of war
but for the human faces   hard to make eye contact

with other gallery goers   we look away   burdened
by what we've seen   a haunted appeal bleeds through
their eyes   tears leaks from mine   all of us complicit

Poem without Huckleberry in it

The first thing I recognise of America is a wide
ribbon of pewter river spreading across the patchwork-
quilted squares of farmer-tilled land below.

It has to be the Mississippi, I think – my first glimpse
of a US icon. 33,000 feet above and the river is so
broad, takes up so much space in the small oval

eye of the plane it has to be kilometres across.
Sinuous, undulant, a cascading dull silver-hued
radiance thrown across the country like a thick thread

of twisted metal appliquéd onto cloth. Someone
has thrown the spool from somewhere up north –
Canada maybe or Minnesota – and the ribbon

has unravelled all the way down the length of the
land, weaving through the middle states, coming
finally to the Gulf of Mexico where the reel runs out.

Traveller's fantasy in Washington DC

A small blue house on New Hampshire Ave –
the kind of blue that calls you in. Long, skinny,

three storeys tall. The doorway is flanked by
two coach lights with flames flickering, even

though it's day. A scarlet crested cardinal –
my first – alights on a branch nearby. Bright

and singular this wet, dull day. He hops onto
the sidewalk, moves to get my attention,

motions me inside… I climb the seven steps
to the front porch. The lock opens to my key turn,

my umbrella slides into the stand. The cadence
of my footfall is familiar to the floorboards

and the house settles into camaraderie. In the
kitchen the blue cup fits my hand. Slipping

into my spot at the bench – I see the courtyard
fogged in rain, dressed in mist. Raindrops swell

to transparent opalescence then fall from the
flowering dogwood. They perfectly offset

the brilliance of the cardinal who has flown
into the yard and sways his tail knowingly.

john and yoko meet for the first time

1966   her avant-garde art
show at a chic london gallery

an apple sells for two hundred
quid   art which taunts

he reckons she's a wanker
high on the ceiling a canvas

he climbs the ladder to read
letters so small he has to use

the magnifying glass hanging
on a chain to read them

later he says that if she had
written *fuck you* he would have

walked out   her philosophy
compressed into a single

affirmative   YES   voiced
against the nihilism of the times

the fashion of smashing pianos
with hammers   of destroying

in the name of art   this tiny
three letter word strikes a spark

which kindles a revolution
kicks off a whole generation

The artist removes the *kopi* of mourning

After seeing *Hold*, an installation by Bridget Nicholson – Winner, Yering Station Sculpture Prize 2016

Bridget smooths wet clay onto my head
gentles it like a bonnet round the bones.
It's a snug fit, a cool soothe of moisture
in the desert of sorrow. Drying, it tightens,
hands holding my bony grief cage. Wordless,
comfort when nothing else helps.

We do mourning so poorly – indigenous
people perfected their way over millennia.
Leaving the cap in place until it fell to pieces,
dust returning to dust. Never disconnected
from their ground of being. Their wisdom
to know how to harness earth's comfort,
connection even at the most unanchored
of times.

The artist gathers women from all cultures
in Gunnedah – indigenous, settler, immigrant –
into a makeshift family. She fashions caps for
each, as personal as fingerprints – the particular
arc and plane of each woman's bone creates
the shape. Each imprinted with her story of loss –
lover, spouse, child, sibling, parent, country,
culture.

She fires the caps in a local kiln. Bone and
ochre-hued. Held upside down, they resemble
bowls or two water-carrying hands joined.
Hung canopied in exhibition, they are 198 life
giving vessels that have not forgotten their genesis
in death, like all begotten life. Jostling they are
eloquent with loss, dynamic with what is still
held.

kopi: clay mourning skullcap

Mother-stone is womb

i.m. EK, remembering a friend, Lake Mungo (Willandra Lakes), NSW

Ankle-deep in history, following your receding, check-shirted
back. Landscape scraped and gouged out of the
rock of the planet – long-dry lake bed, lunettes pitting
the terrain with moon-shaped hollows. Heat makes it
harsh, rises in blurry waves. The sun has flayed the pelt
right off the land, leaving it leather-like; baked and cured

with patches of spilling sand. Trees have no foothold –
there's no shade to shelter under. All I can see is pristine
nature – nothing tells me a human story. Each time I lever
a buried foot free I peel back another decade, another
century, another contested millennium – to you too
short an estimate. Part park ranger, part hierophant, you

turn and say: *our technology,* swinging your arms in an
inclusive 360 arc, *it's all around us!* Your words conjure
modernity, electronica, bamboozling what I think I know.
Underfoot the sand slips again. You're already squatting
ready to give the next lesson. You pick up a hand-sized
rock, point to a mound shaped like the heel of the thumb

on a palm. Bulb of percussion you say proudly, triumphantly,
anointing the bulb with its true technical name. *So much
force*, you say, *and precision to flake a chip the shape and
fineness you want*. You're introducing me to an Aboriginal
Rosetta – text notched and nuanced by human hand, ancient
translation tool. Portal to the long-gone past. You hold

out a handful of flakes, show me how convex fits into concave, as if mother-stone is womb to flake, containing it all in *nuce*. Now I see pieces of worked stone all around us, stone dedicated to specific uses – knives, points, axes, blades. *This a kind of awl for piercing, this a blade for scraping and this would be tied and glued to a spear!*

What I took to be sand dune and random rock has turned into a quarry with workstations and knappers plying their trade, like a cartoon – while I watch it comes to life, morphing into three dimensions, gaining depth of field, veracity.

After Listening to a Ceremony of Carols

Scored for choir and harp. Benjamin Britten, Op. 28 (1942)

It starts; skin-tingling ethereal praise-song.
Sharpened edges rise among harmonies.
Auras of menace pizzicato out from under

the harpist's hands, shorten the distance
between strings and voice, shape the sound
until it has body, substance. Notes surge, urge,

add undercurrents of unease. Between choral
clarity and stringed authority, Britten conjures
the possibility of a christ. Not saccharine or

sentimental. All the beauty you could wish
for without sacrificing muscle of a maverick,
threat of a troublemaker. Music worthy of him.

Heaven backwards

Waiting neighbours catch little Nevaeh, whose name is 'heaven' spelt backwards, Channel 9 News

Everything happens so fast. No
time to think about how flames cut
the sky to shreds like a machete or
how hope balances fear on its blade.

The world shrinks into my neighbour's
shrieks – the baby bundled in her arms,
her face scrunched with terror.

A blanket appears in my hands before
I realise how it got there, before
I register how high the stakes are.

The baby zooms out of the woman's
hands like a football off the boot, no
time to think or judge, arms readied
towards her, ready to catch, to clutch
it to my chest, desperate to be worthy
of this mark.

Later I can't stop seeing the baby
plunge out of the sky. Again and
again, a hundred babies, one after
the other, on crazy replay, perpetual
footy practice session. Catch, clutch,
catch, clutch. All thud into me with
the same almost-winding thwack.
When you know you've got it, a ball
fits into you like it knows its place,
sticks. Never a mark so sweet.

At my father's funeral

Among the worsteds and woollens, the herringbone
weaves and pinstripes. Amongst the navies, the charcoals,

the mission browns. Among bespoke tailoring and off-the-
rack three-piece. Among double and single breasted,

chests – barrel and narrow. Among attire sturdy enough
to stand up without a body inside. Among the solid phalanx

of business suits, row-on-row, shoulder-to-shoulder, the congress
of sober ties nodding discreetly, private understandings, shared

world-view passing wordlessly man-to-man. Among the dark
futility of church pews. Between the cold grief of sandstone,

the implacability of bluestone – the flutter of my psyche's
flimsy fabric – weave open and transparent, shape transmutable.

Colours delicate and mutable. Nothing to anchor cloth to earth,
to tether person to pew. Woven with permeability.

L'informateur

Montigny, Bourgogne, France

The beams – charred, reeking of revenge – remain.
He thought he'd got away with it for another day.
Before he had even the opened the car door – *the coup de grâce*.
Already anticipating sanctuary, his own four stone walls.

He thought he'd got away with it for another day.
The villagers had planned it for months, impossible to forget, forgive.
Already anticipating safety, his own four stone walls.
Always aware of his back, expecting a bullet at any time.

The villagers had planned it for months, impossible to forget, forgive.
He'd despised them, betrayed them, lined his pockets.
Always aware of his back, expecting a bullet at any time.
Douse the bastard with petrol, let him burn like a torch!

He'd despised them, betrayed them, lined his pockets.
Telling himself he couldn't bear his children hollowed with hunger.
Douse the bastard with petrol, burn him like a torch!
He lied, even to himself, couldn't look his wife in the eye.

Soot of hatred, smoke of bitterness spiralling above *le village*.
Before he had even the opened the car door – the *coup de grâce*.
The fire takes all the ancient timbers, thirsty for fuel.
The beams – charred, reeking of revenge – remain.

From the temple's mouth

Abu Simbel, Temple of Rameses II, beloved by Amun, Nubia Egypt

The mouth of the temple is clogged with neglect,
forced to silence by millennial banks of sand.

Drifts first cover the king's stone feet, blown
in by the desolate winds of time. By the sixth

century BC, it is lapping his knees; a slowly
approaching flood which he – mere statue –

is powerless to resist. More centuries pass
until it plugs his mouth, preventing all utterance.

Eventually all the carved and chiselled
attendants, Rameses himself, his queen Nefertari,

even the resplendent gods are rendered mute,
history's forgetting – a silencing. The desert

reclaims the whole massive complex –
buries it beneath huge dunes rising

from the riverbank. The Nile flows on.
Eons of sacredness sealed inside sandstone

walls. Once alive with worshippers
loud with voice, then a giant centuries-old

sarcophagus, biding time. Sand gritty
between the guardian statues' toes,

their stone teeth, it has slipped and slithered
into every crevasse, blocking the passageways,

preventing the sun god from penetrating
to the centre, obscuring the painted stars.

Until Belzoni starts digging. 1817, his second
attempt; this time he knows what to look for.

On his hands and knees, resting during
the sun's violent onslaught. After 24 hours

a pocket opens under his probing. The trapped
years escape with an eloquent whoosh

into the heat-hazed day. Out from the stoppered
silence he hears the sound he has longed

to hear – *the ancient air inside the temple
moaning from its new small mouth.*

This amplitude

Calder Freeway, past Melton, Victoria

Mesmeric miles on bitumen the same steely grey
as the sky. Wispy elongated white-line clouds
flash by. I take the sky highway, steering towards
cumulus, cirrus, getting my bearings from a flock
of galahs happy to lend their gen to a passing
motorist. My vehicle cruises into the stratosphere,
wheels eating air. Landscape shrinks to a painter's
smear on the horizon. The rump of hills is all that's
needed for definition, clefts in their flank – texture.
Everything else is sky – as far and as high as…
Panoramas of light-streaked vapour appear,
avenues of cloud-puff billow. I've joined the
commerce of wind and precipitation, the traffic
of weather. No buildings or street signs break
the day's open invitation. Where have they
been hiding this amplitude? When everything is
pressing in, where have they harboured this haven?

An assay on intimacy

A telephone survey to track flu infection patterns. What did I do yesterday, who did I speak with, touch, allow within arm's reach? Rewriting my day through number and length of contacts, touch, proximity. *How long did it take you to drive from Beacon Lighting to the hospital; were you alone?* He asked, just the right degree of formality, leaving familiarity to me. The minutiae I wouldn't bother sharing with anyone spilled out – *20 minutes from gym to café. I touched 2 people there, 6 came within arm's reach*…a shame my day wasn't more interesting. *Better than most*, he soothed, like a friend trying to put things in perspective. *It would be different*, I said, *if you asked how much of my poem I got written. We should ask everybody that*, he agreed, enthusiastic. I knew he was just asking required questions but it mimicked intimacy. *I know that 7 11!* he exclaimed when I described where I'd stopped for breath mints before tango, seeming pleased that we had it in common. *Did you touch the man who opened the door for you*, he asked like a friend wanting every detail. *He did it because I was all dolled up for tango*, I confided, adding unnecessary detail – the hair, the heels. His probing made me want to open up, give more than asked, a funny combination of hairdresser/counsellor/secular father confessor. It helped me understand reality show contestants. *And of the 8 people at tango how many of those did you touch? The 4 I danced with but I didn't exchange body fluids with any of them!* I couldn't help myself – surely we were friends by now. I almost confessed about the man I'd been fantasising about for weeks, how close he held me, how good his arm felt around my waist, but I held myself back, practicing a last decorum. *And how long did it take you to drive home? And did you have anyone with you?*

The hug

Ordinary enough, not cosy like friends,
or packed with charge like lovers-to-be.
Not melting or merging but unbending –
two trees, boughs briefly touching.

Then a farewelling hand and the gauze
of the car's long dark dust plume. Away
through the green tunnel of aching trees.
Feeling flickering like light through tree-lace,

stronger as I drive on. As if the hug
snags on history – the long, loveless time
since I have been hugged by someone
who means it. Only in the sealed sanctuary

of the car does the hug catch up with me,
quietly insistent like wind's whisper
through leaves, bending my unyielding
trunk, relaxing its hold on distance.

Bach and the essence of things

Lilli Pilli, NSW

'What speaks to us…in Bach…is a strange transfiguration, a breakthrough into the realm of essence…' – Erich Neumann

You're in the cabin playing Bach *Preludes* and *Fugues*
on the harpsichord keyboard, practising those endlessly
repeating themes which plait sounds together in intricate

interweavings. Notes chase each other in ascending aural
spirals, as impossible as Escher's uphill water. Descent is
in rivulets and waves. The sound is spare, simple, but the

music lays down dignity as a fundamental, insists on the
reach of the human spirit, persistence in the face of…as
uplifting as the gums outside – stature tethered to beauty.

*

I'm down on the beach with the cormorants. Long bodies
zoom in from Pelican Island where they've been fishing
and preening all day – their own patch of paradise. Feathers

combed by northerlies, wings hung out to dry, probed by
fingers of sunlight. The birds roost in the gums which circle
the bay. The forest's breath is loam, peat, eucalypt – earthy

intimacy. One bird launches into the space above the water,
flies stately aerial circuits. Another follows, close on its heels.
The birds rise and fall with the thermals, moving in tandem,

then in counterpoint. Dark notes, flying lazy looping fugues
in the gathering dusk, chasing what is elusive to humans.
The sky pours an avalanche of colour into the waiting ocean.

*

We have our own versions of the fugue, moving contrapuntally
and in tandem, like the music. Now you play, I listen, filled with
reverence at the sounds which emerge from your hands, hands

which know the keyboard so intimately, know me likewise…
That a human could compose this pure, liquid simplicity…that
you could coax beauty out from where it lies latent – in notes

on the page, the keyboard, your own dexterity and whole heart.
True to the chase, like Bach was. It's all here, the music says,
the essence of everything dear, drenching this very moment.

Playing the Soft-loud

January 2016, Lilli Pilli, NSW
George Frideric Handel, Oboe Sonatas in C minor and G
Robert Schumann, Romances 1 & 3, Op 94 for piano and oboe

You lay down lines of notes in neural pathways
you can return to, backtrack to get runs right,
figure out where to put your fingers, find melodies,
rhythms. Listening to you learn new pieces is like sitting
at the composer's elbow; hearing him make music

from ideas. Wrong notes, clunky cadences
just part of learning. On first practice, small patches
of coherence emerge. Each piece's rationale is yet
to be revealed, but each repeat undoes a knot, allows
the spool of sound to unravel without getting stuck.

*

> The lazy day unfolds. Rain glazes
> maculata gum trunks, turns them
> from cream to muted lime – shockingly
>
> fluorescent – more shades to the forest
> palette of palm, fern, eucalypt. Even
> the light, this misty day – green-tinged.

*

The patches of coherence lengthen as themes
are revealed. Exciting to recognise repeated motifs,
to imagine the composer finding multiple places
for his signature melodies. Was it laborious? Joyful?
Phrases take on different guises depending on their

surroundings. Learning the Handel is easier, you say –
Baroque predictability. Only small wrinkles still
to iron out. The Romances are emotional, volatile,
difficult to predict how they come together, where
they will go. Let alone the mania Schumann suffered

while writing them. Plaintive strains amongst the lyric;
his voice, lamenting. A gift for Clara; Christmas 1848.
He makes an attempt on his life five years later, puts
himself in the asylum where he dies two years after
that. Despite upbeat passages, all the tragedy leaks

out of the music. I want to put a comforting hand
on his shoulder. You grapple, and your musical
intelligence prevails. I quicken to hear the heart
of each piece emerge, like sculpture from the woodblock,
more true and fine the further the sculptor goes.

*

>The next day, birds – happy,
>it seems the deluge has finally
>ceased. The maculata are paler,
>
>more flesh-like. Tall and stately
>like the Handel. Rising from
>the dead, as Rilke says.

*

You have the Handel now, fingering pencilled
on the score. The Romances are still difficult –
you play right-hand-only to straighten complicated
sequences. The whole is disparate, unresolved,

not fulfilling that first gorgeous opening phrase's
promise. By session's end, you say they're in you now;
your brain, your hands. Some poets say that poems live
like this; in the poet's hands, ready to play onto paper.

*

> A golden whistler in a clean
> white bib marks the occasion,
>
> flies repeatedly against the glass,
> gently knocking, knocking.

The filament of the body

'In speed we hurl ourselves beyond the body' – T.E. Lawrence

From the bike, clouds scud silently across a muted sky. Long sustained,
sometimes vibrato notes played to an audience of mountains and trees.
Wind paints colour on the sky's immaculate ceiling; imprinting the canvas,

like landscape imprints the motorcycling body. A mountain's height
and girth write contour lines on a map. Riding pillion they become
degrees of lean and rock-a-bye motion. Ascent is incremental – traversing

the vertiginous side of the slope, then manoeuvring switch-back bends
when the bike doubles on itself, slows to almost stalling speed. Momentum
and sticky tyres keep us from bitumen. We leap out of the corner in

a flamboyant burst of acceleration. Adrenaline floods, fizzes along synapses.
Fear and delight open and close me, my sometimes antagonistic fellow
travellers. On the flat, we meander across flood-plains, movement as fluid

as river, as liquid as untethered thought. Both of us part of a single flow.
The rider shrinks to a pinpoint of concentrated vigilance, expands into
multiple pathways of muscular memory, rides them in taut practiced

concert. We weight and unweight in balletic grace – *we are not earthbound.*
I lurch between trust and panic at my total lack of control.
Plunged into the body then, alchemically, beyond it again. On the ground

but flying; the whoosh as wind rushes past. We keep pace with the birds,
nothing but a thin shell of helmet-plastic between us and them. *Not the
conquest of air but our entry thither.* Landscape's physicality, feelings'

pitted, porous surface, their substance and tangibility, registered
together in the body's fine-tuned filament. And beyond –
speed, infinite sky, transcendence – all part of a single flow.

Riding back in the dusk

Malmsbury, Victoria

There's no black like
the black of trees

silhouetted against sunset;
matt, boot-black black.

Baked-on Bakelite black,
backlit by the sky's citrus

tones – mandarin, orange
and lemon morphing

into persimmon-red,
magenta. The colours

zing into the sky, into
the eager eye. Light flares

out as through an aperture,
intensified by restriction.

Tonight, riding in tandem
through the blazing dark,

we're on the threshold,
peering into a lit room

through a horizon-long
chink of light. Later,

liminal, bodies blazing,

we move in tandem
in that illuminated room.

The ghost of an argument

'Liebchen, / with whom should I quarrel except in the hiss of love, / that harsh, irregular flame?' – Stanley Kunitz

Coming into the room next morning
the air retains a residue of disturbance,

molecules vibrating at a fast though
no longer furious rate. The couches

remain facing each other as they were
when we left them last night. They

haven't softened in the dark as we
did, the small one sliding into the

spoon of the larger, the bigger curling
into the arm-crook of the smaller.

Calling the world into being

for Billie Sheila Bailey

'Marvelous Truth, confront us / at every turn, / in every guise, iron ball, / egg, dark horse, shadow, cloud / of breath on the air, / dwell/ in our crowded hearts' – from *Matins*, Denise Levertov

Hooked to my hip, held close, you lean in to me, listening.
Your ears – small pink shells – furl into you, open you out

into the waiting world. My voice is pitched just for you,
a low steady rumble of reassurance amidst the clatter

of crockery, the buzz of conversation and coffee-making,
stilling the fidgets and squirms of your one-year-old insatiability

in the teeming world. Things clamour, demand contact –
your newness of having and taking, of taste – your principal

method to assay worth. You are primal, driven; a wriggling
delight to witness, challenge to divert. This time we walk

a café circuit – fridge to serving-hatch to coffee machine
and back again. *Bottled water, mineral water, flavoured water*,

I say, stopping in front of stacked shelves, indicating each row
of bottles in turn, *juice, coconut water, jam*. Your eyes

follow my pointing finger as I say the mantra. You never stir;
never reach with your eyes or hands after the next new thing.

We're practicing attentiveness, soft focus; poet skills I'm thrilled
to pass on. I call the thing into the space between us, invoke it

by repeating its humble name: *coffee machine, cup, sugar*.
Freed from competition with the plethora, they come into

their own selves, distinct, vibrating with simple presence.
We've entered the place where things respond to hallowing:

plate, chef, pancakes; a sacred act which holds us together
in the present moment, time stretching long between us.

Embarking together

for JB

When all the day's words have
been said, laughs and wrangles

done, the swinging hammock
of the mind slows. Day's

divestment begins – my knees
under your tummy, your hand

holding a curve of my breast.
The sweetness of closing

the day with you. That there
is a you to share it with, that

that you, is you. Burrowing
under blankets, our bodies

flank to flank, making animal
warmth. Putting aside costumes,

cognition, the complicated
algorithms of daily life, to sink

into simple bodily existence.
Your breath warm on my neck.

The joy of riding the breath
wave all the way to shore.

Peeling apart – our own dream
or worry-swaddled sides of the

bed for sleep. Deep unknowingness
embarked upon together.

Epilogue

…not to give shape to sound but sound to give shape to silence

( )

Nestled in the space
between one note

        and the next. At the end
        of the phrase, the stave.

Before the next instrument
throws its voice into the

        auditorium. At the end
        of the piece, before the

applause, coloured by the relief
and grief of finitude. Briefly,

        at the end of the poetic
        line, longer at the end

of the sentence, the stanza.
Hidden in plain view

        in the page's white space.
        After the engine's throat

closes, the chainsaw's
racket fades. After the last

        bird farewells the day.
        After a breath, a life…

Notes

'Matti ka attar': Isabel (Joy) Bear received a Member of the Order of Australia for her services to science. She retired in 2015 aged 88. She and Richard Thomas from CSIRO discovered and named the chemical processes which produce the scent of rain: Petrichor. It is produced in Lucknow, India, as *Matti ka attar.*

'Poem without Huckelbury in it': the word Mississippi comes from the Ojibwe word *misi-ziibi*, 'Great River'.

'The artist removes the *Kopi* of mourning': (Aboriginal) women would cover their heads in clay when someone died. Their period of mourning was defined by the length of time it took for the clay to crack and disintegrate. (Robert Horne, Curator, Cumbo Gunnerah Museum, Gunnedah, NSW)

'The filament of the body': quotes from T.E. Lawrence *Confessions of Faith*

'From the temple's mouth': story and quote from Anne Michaels's *The Winter Vault*

Acknowledgements

With deep thanks to the poetry friends who have given feedback and critique and aided my development as a poet – Sue Lockwood, Alice White, Diane Fahey, Anne Elvey and Susan Fealy.

I would like to thank the editors of the following journals for publishing poems, sometimes in different versions.

'An assay on intimacy,' 'A poem without Hucklebury in it', *Otoliths*
'Exuviate', 'The marmalade fox', & 'Going to the holy trees', *Poetry Monash*
'Ground and air spangled', *Scriturra,* Number 3, Spring 2016
'Had I the Heaven's cloths', *Otoliths,* Issue 40, Southern Summer 2016
'Harvesting sweet pea seeds', *Otoliths,* Issue 37, Southern Autumn, 2015
'Heaven backward', *Live Encounters*, Indonesia, 2017
'In circlets of dusky light', *Pennsylvania Review,* USA, Spring 2017
'*L'Informateur*': *The French Literary Review*, 2014, France
':meditations on melancholy', *Australian Poetry Journal*, Vol. 5 Issue 1, 2015 & *Yula*, 2014
'Old friends, three elementals', *Sentinel Literary Quarterly*, UK, October 2016
'Pocket and seed', *Deep Water Literary Journal*, Ireland, 2014 & 'The empty chairs', 2016
'Riding back in the dusk', *Verity la*, July 2015
'Swiftlet Hotel', *Famous Reporter* 44, 2012
'The filament of the body', *Westerly* 61:2, November 2016
'The hug', *Blue Giraffe*, 2015
'This amplitude', *Blue Pepper*, October 2015
'Two green parrots', *Plumwood Mountain,* July 2014, 'On being taken there', *Plumwood Mountain,* January 2015, 'Golden every wych way', *Plumwood Mountain,* September 2015, 'Elegy for a tree', *Plumwood Mountain,* January 2016,
'The river beneath', *Antithesis, 2016*

With thanks to the editors of the following anthologies for publishing my work:

(   ), 'ear to earth', *Henry Kendall Anthology*, 2017

'Arboreal sorority', *New Shoots Anthology*, Red Room, 2017

':mediations on melancholy' & 'Axiology', *The fractured self*, edited by Heather Taylor Johnston, UQP, 2017

'Harvesting sweet pea pods', & 'Riding back in the dusk', *Australian Poetry Journal Members Anthology*

The following poems were awarded in competitions, with thanks to the judges:

'Arboreal Sorority,' Shortlisted, *New Shoots*, NSW, 2017

'Black Kites Broome', Longlisted, Lane Cover Poetry Prize, 2016

'Cockatoo: A Cautionary', Shortlisted and commended, Melbourne Poets Union International Poetry Prize, 2015

'Bach and the essence of things', Shortlisted, Ron Pretty Poetry Prize 2015, published on website

'Motherstone is womb', Longlisted, Canberra University Vice Chancellor's International Poetry Prize, 2015

With thanks to the following curators for exhibiting my work:

'Before the day's push and grab', *The Wall*, Poland

'Bodies remembering war', The George Paton Gallery, Text and Word based exhibition, August 2017

www.ingramcontent.com/pod-product-compliance
Lightning Source LLC
Chambersburg PA
CBHW062145100526
44589CB00014B/1694